On the

SOCCER TEAMS
FROM AROUND THE WORLD

MEGAN COOLEY PETERSON

BLACK
RABBIT
BOOKS

Bolt is published by Black Rabbit Books
P.O. Box 3263, Mankato, Minnesota, 56002.
www.blackrabbitbooks.com
Copyright © 2018 Black Rabbit Books

Marysa Storm, editor; Michael Sellner, designer;
Omay Ayres, photo researcher

Library of Congress Cataloging-in-Publication Data
Peterson, Megan Cooley, author.
Soccer teams from around the world / by Megan Cooley Peterson.
Mankato, Minnesota : Black Rabbit Books, 2018. | Series: Bolt.
On the pitch | Audience: Age 9-12. | Audience: Grade 4 to 6. | Includes
bibliographical references and index.
LCCN 2016049975 (print) | LCCN 2016057438 (ebook)
ISBN 9781680721706 (library binding) | ISBN 9781680722345 (e-book) |
ISBN 9781680724677 (paperback)
LCSH: Soccer teams–Juvenile literature.
Soccer–History–Juvenile literature.
LCC GV943.25 .P477 2016 (print) | LCC GV943.25 (ebook)
DDC 796.334–dc23
LC record available at https://lccn.loc.gov/2016049975

Printed in the United States at CG Book Printers,
North Mankato, Minnesota, 56003. 3/17

Image Credits

Contents

CHAPTER 1

Teamwork

Forwards score lightning-fast goals. **Defenders** steal the ball. Goalkeepers make diving saves. Fans cheer loudly.

Soccer teams make fans proud. Take a closer look at some popular teams around the world.

WORLD SOCCER

Confederations oversee soccer in different parts of the world.

CAF
Confederation of African Football

CONCACAF
Confederation of North, Central American, and Caribbean Association Football

CONMEBOL
South American Football Confederation

UEFA
Union of
European Football
Associations

OFC
Oceania Football
Confederation

AFC
Asian Football
Confederation

CHAPTER 2

Club Teams

Club teams compete in **leagues**.

Each league has many teams.

Arsenal

League: Premier League, England

Arsenal is a famous men's team. From 2003 to 2004, it played 49 league games without losing. This number is a record for English teams.

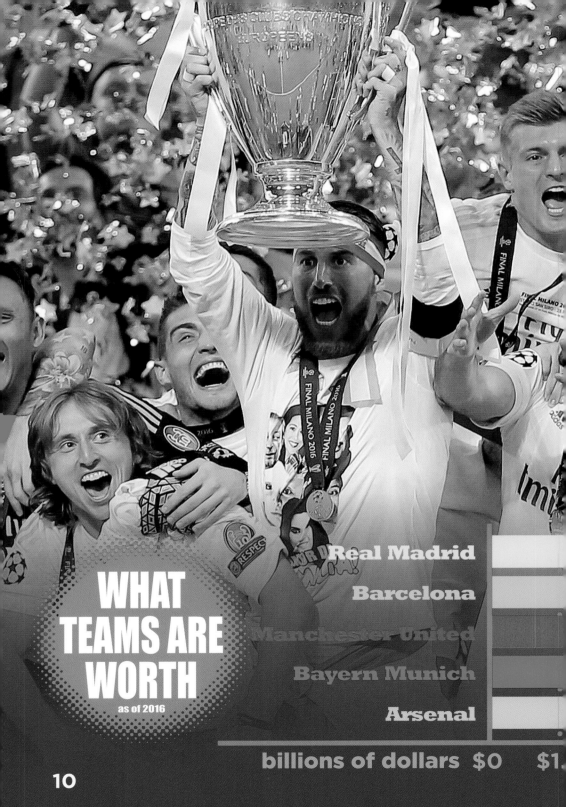

WHAT TEAMS ARE WORTH
as of 2016

Real Madrid
Barcelona
Manchester United
Bayern Munich
Arsenal

billions of dollars $0 $1.

Real Madrid
League: La Liga, Spain

FIFA named Real Madrid the best club of the 20th century. It's not surprising. The team has won 11 championships.

The UEFA Champions League is the biggest club contest. Winners get the Champions League trophy.

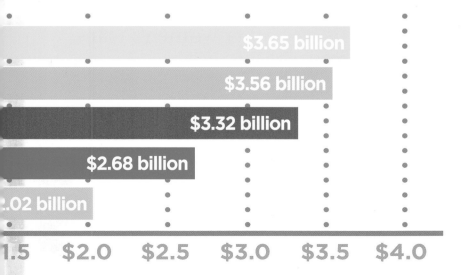

$3.65 billion
$3.56 billion
$3.32 billion
$2.68 billion
.02 billion

1.5 $2.0 $2.5 $3.0 $3.5 $4.0

FFC Frankfurt

League: Women's Bundesliga, Germany

FFC Frankfurt is a tough team. The players have skilled footwork. The team has excellent goalkeeping. They have four Champions League trophies. This number is more than any other women's team.

Bayern Munich

League:
Men's Bundesliga,
Germany

Bayern Munich is one of Germany's most popular clubs. In the 2012–2013 season, the team earned a **treble**. It won the league and the German Cup. It also won the Champions League.

Champions League Wins
as of 2016

Real Madrid
11

Milan
7

Barcelona
5

Bayern Munich
5

Liverpool
5

Ajax
4

FFC Frankfurt
4

Chelsea

League: Premier League, England

In 2012, Chelsea beat Bayern Munich 4–3. This win happened during a **penalty shoot-out**. It was the team's first Champions League trophy. The team also has four Premier League titles.

Soccer is called football in many parts of the world. The field is often called a pitch.

Barcelona
League: La Liga, Spain

Barcelona has a strong defense. It stops many goals. The team's playing style works. It has won five Champions League trophies.

Barcelona and Real Madrid are rivals. Matches between them are a big deal.

Club Teams

Chelsea
forms.

Barcelona
forms.

1899

1886

1900

1902

1905

1956

Arsenal
forms.

Bayern Munich
forms.

Real Madrid
forms.

Bayern Munich wins its fifth Champions League trophy.

Barcelona wins its first Champions League trophy.

Real Madrid wins its 11th Champions League trophy.

1992

2013

2016

1998

2015

FFC Frankfurt forms.

Barcelona wins its fifth Champions League trophy. FFC Frankfurt takes home its fourth Champions League trophy.

Real Madrid wins its first Champions League trophy.

CHAPTER 3

National

National teams compete for the World Cup. The Cup is soccer's top prize. Each country has one national team. There is a World Cup for men and for women.

Italy

Italy's men's team has done well at the World Cup. Italy was the first European team to win. It won the World Cup in 1934. Since then, it's won three more times.

LONGEST WINNING STREAKS IN INTERNATIONAL GAMES

United States (women)	Spain (men)	Brazil (men)	Argentina (men)	France (men)	Italy (men)
42 matches	35 matches	35 matches	31 matches	30 matches	30 matches
2012–2014	2007–2009	1993–1996	1991–1993	1994–1996	1935–1939

The U.S. women's team also rules the Olympics. It has won the gold medal four times. It took home gold in 1996, 2004, 2008, and 2012.

United States

For years, women could not play in the World Cup. The first Women's World Cup was in 1991. The United States won. It beat Norway 2–1.

The U.S. women's team has become powerful. Players pick apart defenses. They play well under pressure.

Germany

Germany has talented national teams. The women's team won the World Cup twice. They won in 2003 and 2007. The men's team has four titles. There is a lot of young talent on these teams. Experienced players help them win too.

as of 2016

Brazil
(men's team) years won: **195**

Germany
(men's team) years won: **195**

Italy
(men's team) years won: **193**

United States
(women's team) years won: **199**

Germany
(women's team) years won: **200**

Norway
(women's team) years won: **199**

Japan
(women's team) years won: **201**

1962 1970 1994 2002 **5**

1974 1990 2014 **4**

1938 1982 2006 **4**

1999 2015 **3**

2007 **2**

Brazil

Brazil's men's team may be the best. It has won five World Cups. That is more than any other team. It's played in every World Cup tournament. It is the only team that has done so.

Soccer's best teams set records. They entertain millions of fans. Which team will you cheer for?

GLOSSARY

confederation (KON-fed-ur-ay-shun)—a group of soccer teams that help organize tournaments

defender (de-FEN-dur)—a player who works to stop the other team from scoring

FIFA—International Federation of Association Football; FIFA controls world soccer.

forward (FOR-wurd)—a soccer player whose main job is to move the ball toward the opponent's goal and try to score

league (LEEG)—a group of sports teams that play against each other

penalty (PEN-uhl-tee)—a punishment for breaking the rules

rival (RYE-vuhl)—someone competing for the same thing as someone else

shoot-out (SHOOT-owt)—a method of breaking a tie score at the end of overtime play

tournament (TUR-nuh-muhnt)—a series of matches between several teams, ending in one winner

treble (TREB-uhl)—winning a league title, a main national cup, and the Champions League in one season

BOOKS

Jankowski, Emily. *Soccer's Greatest Records*. Greatest Records in Sports. New York: PowerKids Press, 2015.

Rausch, David. *Major League Soccer*. Major League Sports. Minneapolis: Bellwether Media, Inc., 2015.

Whiting, Jim. *FC Barcelona*. European Soccer. Mankato, MN: Creative Education, 2015.

WEBSITES

History of FIFA - The First FIFA World Cup
www.fifa.com/about-fifa/who-we-are/history/first-fifa-world-cup.html

Premier League
www.premierleague.com/en-gb.html

Soccer (Football)
www.ducksters.com/sports/soccer.php

INDEX